October 2011

INFORMATION SECURITY

Weaknesses Continue Amid New Federal Efforts to Implement Requirements

INFORMATION SECURITY

Weaknesses Continue Amid New Federal Efforts to Implement Requirements

Highlights of GAO-12-137, a report to congressional committees

Why GAO Did This Study

For many years, GAO has reported that weaknesses in information security can lead to serious consequences—such as intrusions by malicious individuals, compromised networks, and the theft of sensitive information including personally identifiable information—and has identified information security as a governmentwide high-risk area. The Federal Information Security Management Act of 2002 (FISMA) established information security program, evaluation, and annual reporting requirements for federal agencies. The act requires the Office of Management and Budget (OMB) to oversee and report to Congress on agency information security policies and practices, including agencies' compliance with FISMA.

FISMA also requires that GAO periodically report to Congress on (1) the adequacy and effectiveness of agencies' information security policies and practices and (2) agencies' implementation of FISMA requirements. To do this, GAO analyzed information security-related reports and data from 24 major federal agencies, their inspectors general, OMB, and GAO.

What GAO Recommends

GAO is recommending that the Director of OMB provide performance targets for metrics included in OMB's annual FISMA reporting instructions to agencies and inspectors general. OMB stated it was more appropriate for those targets to be included in the performance metrics that are now issued separately by the Department of Homeland Security. GAO agrees that this meets the intent of its recommendation.

View GAO-12-137. For more information, contact Gregory C.Wilshusen at (202) 512-6244 or wilshuseng@gao.gov.

What GAO Found

Weaknesses in information security policies and practices at 24 major federal agencies continue to place the confidentiality, integrity, and availability of sensitive information and information systems at risk. Consistent with this risk, reports of security incidents from federal agencies are on the rise, increasing over 650 percent over the past 5 years. Each of the 24 agencies reviewed had weaknesses in information security controls (see figure). An underlying reason for these weaknesses is that agencies have not fully implemented their information security programs. As a result, they have limited assurance that controls are in place and operating as intended to protect their information resources, thereby leaving them vulnerable to attack or compromise. In reports for fiscal years 2010 and 2011, GAO and agency inspectors general have made hundreds of recommendations to agencies for actions necessary to resolve control deficiencies and information security program shortfalls. Agencies generally agreed with most of GAO's recommendations and indicated that they would implement them.

Information Security Weaknesses at Major Federal Agencies for Fiscal Year 2010
Number of agencies

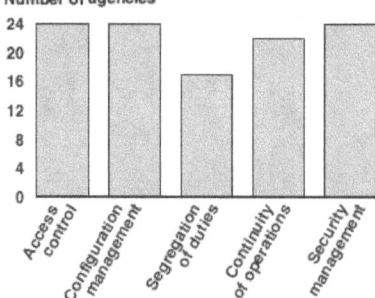

Information security weakness category

Source: GAO analysis of agency, inspectors general, and GAO reports.

OMB, agencies, and the National Institute of Standards and Technology took actions intended to improve the implementation of security requirements, but more work is necessary. Beginning in fiscal year 2009, OMB provided agencies with a new online tool to report their information security postures and, in fiscal year 2010, instituted the use of new and revised metrics. Nevertheless, OMB's guidance for those metrics did not always provide performance targets for measuring improvement. In addition, weaknesses were identified in the processes agencies used to implement requirements. Specifically, agencies did not always ensure (1) personnel with significant responsibilities received training; (2) security controls were monitored continuously; (3) weaknesses were remediated effectively; and (4) incidents were resolved in a timely manner, among other areas. Until hundreds of recommendations are implemented and program weaknesses are corrected, agencies will continue to face challenges in securing their information and information systems.

_____ United States Government Accountability Office

Contents

Abbreviations

DHS	Department of Homeland Security
FISMA	Federal Information Security Management Act of 2002
NIST	National Institute of Standards and Technology
OMB	Office of Management and Budget
POA&M	Plan of Action and Milestones
US-CERT	United States Computer Emergency Readiness Team

United States Government Accountability Office
Washington, DC 20548

October 3, 2011

The Honorable Joseph I. Lieberman
Chairman
The Honorable Susan M. Collins
Ranking Member
Committee on Homeland Security and Governmental Affairs
United States Senate

The Honorable Darrell E. Issa
Chairman
The Honorable Elijah E. Cummings
Ranking Member
Committee on Oversight and Government Reform
House of Representatives

Threats to systems supporting critical infrastructure and federal information systems are evolving and growing. For example, advanced persistent threats—where an adversary that possesses sophisticated levels of expertise and significant resources can attack by using multiple means such as cyber, physical, or deception to achieve its objectives—pose increasing risks. The Director of National Intelligence has warned of the increasing globalization of cyber attacks, from foreign militaries to organized international crime. In February 2011, he testified that there had been a dramatic increase in malicious cyber activity targeting U.S. computers and networks, including a more than tripling of the volume of malicious software since 2009.[1] In this increasingly challenging and hostile environment, federal agencies remain at risk as threats are evolving in ways that require innovative, coordinated, and sustained responses across the U.S. government.

The Federal Information Security Management Act (FISMA) of 2002 established current information security program, evaluation, and reporting requirements for federal agencies. FISMA requires federal agencies, the Office of Management and Budget (OMB), and the National Institute of Standards and Technology (NIST) to prepare annual reports.

---

[1]Director of National Intelligence, Worldwide Threat Assessment of the U.S. Intelligence Community, statement for the record, Senate Select Committee on Intelligence (Washington, D.C.: Feb. 16, 2011).

FISMA also includes a requirement for independent annual evaluations by the agencies' inspectors general or independent external auditors.

In accordance with FISMA's requirement that GAO periodically report to Congress, our objectives were to evaluate (1) the adequacy and effectiveness of agencies' information security policies and practices and (2) federal agencies' implementation of FISMA requirements. To accomplish these objectives, we analyzed our information security reports as well as those from 24 major federal agencies,[2] their offices of inspector general, and OMB. We also conducted interviews with agency officials at selected agencies. Where possible, we categorized findings from those reports into security control areas defined by FISMA and our Federal Information System Controls Audit Manual.[3]

We conducted this performance audit from September 2010 to October 2011 in accordance with generally accepted government auditing standards. Those standards require that we plan and perform the audit to obtain sufficient, appropriate evidence to provide a reasonable basis for our findings and conclusions based on our audit objectives. We believe that the evidence obtained provides a reasonable basis for our findings and conclusions based on our audit objectives. For more details on our objectives, scope, and methodology, see appendix I.

Background

To help protect against threats to federal systems, FISMA sets forth a comprehensive framework for ensuring the effectiveness of information security controls over information resources that support federal operations and assets. Its framework creates a cycle of risk management activities necessary for an effective security program. It is also intended to provide a mechanism for improved oversight of federal agency information security programs.

---

[2]The 24 major departments and agencies are the Departments of Agriculture, Commerce, Defense, Education, Energy, Health and Human Services, Homeland Security, Housing and Urban Development, the Interior, Justice, Labor, State, Transportation, the Treasury, and Veterans Affairs; the Environmental Protection Agency, General Services Administration, National Aeronautics and Space Administration, National Science Foundation, Nuclear Regulatory Commission, Office of Personnel Management, Small Business Administration, Social Security Administration, and U.S. Agency for International Development.

[3]GAO, *Federal Information System Controls Audit Manual (FISCAM),* GAO-09-232G (Washington, D.C.: February 2009).

In order to ensure the implementation of this framework, FISMA assigns specific responsibilities to (1) OMB, to develop and oversee the implementation of policies, principles, standards, and guidelines on information security; to report, at least annually, on agency compliance with the act; and to approve or disapprove, agency information security programs; (2) agency heads, to provide information security protections commensurate with the risk and magnitude of the harm resulting from unauthorized access, use, disclosure, disruption, modification, or destruction of information collected or maintained by or on behalf of the agency; (3) agency heads and chief information officers, to develop, document, and implement an agencywide information security program, among others; (4) inspectors general, to conduct annual independent evaluations of agency efforts to effectively implement information security; and (5) NIST to provide standards and guidance to agencies on information security.

FISMA also assigns responsibility to OMB for ensuring the operation of a federal information security incident center. The required functions of this center are performed by the Department of Homeland Security's (DHS) United States Computer Emergency Readiness Team (US-CERT), which was established to aggregate and disseminate cybersecurity information to improve warning and response to incidents, increase coordination of response information, reduce vulnerabilities, and enhance prevention and protection. In addition, the act requires each agency to report annually to OMB, selected congressional committees, and the Comptroller General on the adequacy of its information security policies, procedures, practices, and compliance with requirements. FISMA also requires OMB to report annually to Congress by March 1. See appendix II for additional information on the responsibilities of each entity.

Weaknesses in Information Security Place Sensitive Information and Information Systems at Risk

Federal agencies' information and information systems remain at risk. This risk is illustrated in part by the rising numbers of incidents reported by federal agencies in fiscal year 2010. At the same time, weaknesses in their information security policies and practices compromised their efforts to protect against threats. Furthermore, our work and reviews by inspectors general highlight information security control deficiencies at agencies that expose information and information systems supporting federal operations and assets to elevated risk of unauthorized use, disclosure, modification, and disruption. Accordingly, we and agency inspectors general have made hundreds of recommendations to agencies in fiscal years 2010 and 2011 to address these security control deficiencies.

The Number of Incidents Reported by Federal Agencies Continues to Rise

Federal agencies have reported increasing numbers of security incidents that placed sensitive information at risk. When incidents occur, agencies are to notify the federal information security incident center—US-CERT. Over the past 5 years, the number of incidents reported by federal agencies to US-CERT has increased from 5,503 incidents in fiscal year 2006 to 41,776 incidents in fiscal year 2010, an increase of over 650 percent (see fig.1).[4]

Figure 1: Incidents Reported to US-CERT, Fiscal Years 2006-2010

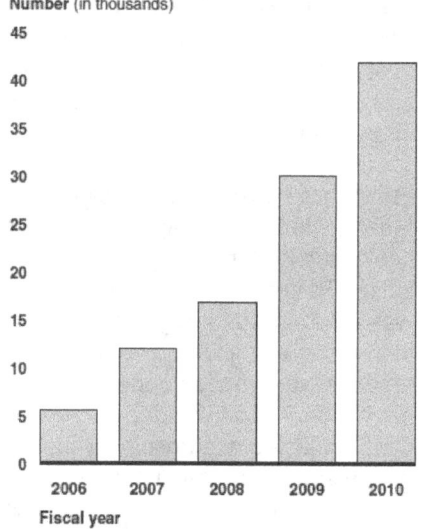

Number (in thousands)

Fiscal year

Source: GAO analysis of US-CERT data.

Agencies also reported the following types of incidents and events based on US-CERT-defined categories:

- **Unauthorized access:** Gaining logical or physical access to a federal agency's network, system, application, data, or other resource without permission.

---

[4]According to US-CERT, the growth in the gross number of incidents is attributable, at least in part, to agencies improving detection of security incidents on their respective networks, and then possibly implementing appropriate responsive and preventative countermeasures.

- **Denial of service:** Preventing or impairing the normal authorized functionality of networks, systems, or applications by exhausting resources. This activity includes being the victim of or participating in a denial of service attack.

- **Malicious code:** Installing malicious software (e.g., virus, worm, Trojan horse, or other code-based malicious entity) that infects an operating system or application. Agencies are not required to report malicious logic that has been successfully quarantined by antivirus software.

- **Improper usage:** Violating acceptable computing use policies.

- **Scans/probes/attempted access:** Accessing or identifying a federal agency computer, open ports, protocols, service, or any combination of these for later exploit. This activity does not directly result in a compromise or denial of service.

- **Unconfirmed incidents under investigation:** Investigating unconfirmed incidents that are potentially malicious or anomalous activity deemed by the reporting entity to warrant further review. According to DHS officials, these incidents include those that US-CERT detects through its intrusion detection system, supplemented by agency reports for investigation.

As indicated in figure 2, the four most prevalent types of incidents and events reported to US-CERT during fiscal year 2010 were: (1) malicious code; (2) unconfirmed incidents under investigation; (3) improper usage; and (4) unauthorized access.

Figure 2: Types of Incidents Reported to US-CERT in Fiscal Year 2010 by Category

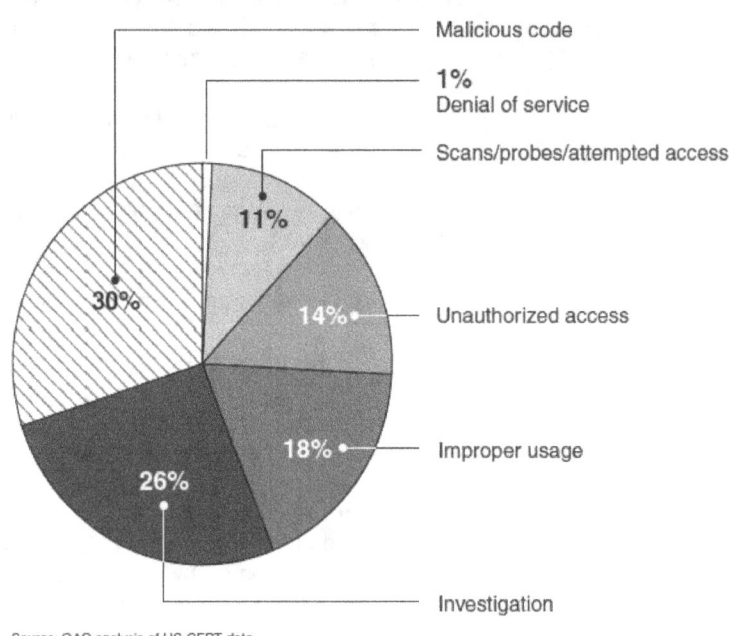

Malicious code

1%
Denial of service

Scans/probes/attempted access

11%

30%

14% — Unauthorized access

18% — Improper usage

26%

Investigation

Source: GAO analysis of US-CERT data.

Reported attacks and unintentional incidents involving federal systems and critical infrastructure systems demonstrate that a serious attack could be devastating. Agencies have experienced a wide range of incidents involving data loss or theft, computer intrusions, and privacy breaches, underscoring the need for improved security practices. The following examples, included to reflect incidents reported in 2010 and 2011, illustrate that a broad array of information and assets remain at risk.

- An employee at federal financial institution downloaded unauthorized accounting source code to a bank hard drive which he had previously reported as stolen. The institution's internal security personnel are investigating and believe the bank employee may have shared the code with a student in another country.

- A well-known hacker group, according to an online news journal, was planning a cyber protest attack on a federal agency, using mobile phones and massive crowds of supporters as well as online supporters. This attack was intended to slow or stop traffic in and out of the agency and delay operations.

- A user on a department's network was tricked by a carefully crafted e-mail to go to a website on the pretense that he had won a new car in a lottery he supposedly entered by answering some simple questions about his pets. Later, he found that several credit cards had been opened in his name and large amounts of pet supplies had been ordered without his knowledge.

- A contractor working for a federal agency sent an unencrypted e-mail from his workstation to his personal e-mail account. This was detected by a monitoring tool at the agency and an immediate investigation was initiated. Several agency personnel had their personal information sent in an unencrypted e-mail to an unauthorized account.

- Network security personnel at a federal institution noted that a large number of network probes on their system originated from an underground hacking group. The institution contacted US-CERT and asked that it contact the service provider to request that the IP address be blocked so that it could no longer probe the institution.

- A federal agency's website was reportedly attacked by a hacker group. Initial analysis determined the hack took place via a web implementation of Java. The attackers have not completely taken down the web server; however, considerable peaks of traffic have been detected.

Information Security Control Deficiencies Place Federal Operations and Assets at Risk

Our audits have identified information security deficiencies in both financial and nonfinancial systems, including vulnerabilities in federal systems. We have made hundreds of recommendations to agencies in fiscal years 2010 and 2011 to address these security control deficiencies. However, most of these recommendations have not yet been fully implemented. The following examples, reported in 2010 and 2011, describe the risks we found at federal agencies, our recommendations, and the actions the agencies plan to take.

- In March 2011, we reported that the Internal Revenue Service had made progress in correcting previously reported information security weaknesses, but a significant number of them remained unresolved or unmitigated.[5] For example, the agency did not sufficiently (1) restrict users' access to databases to only the access needed to perform their jobs; (2) secure the system it uses to support and manage its computer access request, approval, and review processes; (3) update database software residing on servers that support its general ledger system; and (4) enable certain auditing features on databases supporting financial and tax processing systems. An underlying reason for these weaknesses was that the Internal Revenue Service had not yet fully implemented required components of its comprehensive information security program. As a result, financial and taxpayer information remain unnecessarily vulnerable to insider threats and at increased risk of unauthorized disclosure, modification, or destruction; financial data are at increased risk of errors that result in misstatement; and the agency's management decisions may be based on unreliable or inaccurate financial information. We recommended that the Internal Revenue Service take 32 specific actions for correcting newly identified control weaknesses, and it agreed to develop a detailed corrective action plan that addresses them.

- In November 2010, we reported that the Federal Deposit Insurance Corporation did not sufficiently implement access and other controls intended to protect the confidentiality, integrity, and availability of its financial systems and information.[6] For example, it did not always (1) sufficiently restrict user access to systems; (2) ensure strong system boundaries; (3) consistently enforce strong controls for identifying and authenticating users; (4) encrypt sensitive information; or (5) audit and monitor security-relevant events. In addition, the Federal Deposit Insurance Corporation did not have policies, procedures, and controls in place to ensure the appropriate segregation of incompatible duties, adequately manage the configuration of its financial information systems, and update contingency plans. An underlying reason for these weaknesses was that the corporation did not always fully implement several information security program activities, such as effectively developing, documenting, and implementing security

---

[5]GAO, *Information Security: IRS Needs to Enhance Internal Control over Financial Reporting and Taxpayer Data*, GAO-11-308 (Washington, D.C.: Mar.15, 2011).

[6]GAO, *Information Security: Federal Deposit Insurance Corporation Needs to Mitigate Control Weaknesses,* GAO-11-29 (Washington, D.C.: Nov. 30, 2010).

policies. As a result, it faced an elevated risk of the misuse of federal assets, unauthorized modification or destruction of financial information, inappropriate disclosure of other sensitive information, and disruption of computer operations. Accordingly, we recommended that the corporation fully implement several key activities to enhance its information security program. The Federal Deposit Insurance Corporation generally agreed with our recommendations and stated that it planned to address the identified weaknesses.

- In October 2010, we reported that the National Archives and Records Administration had not effectively implemented information security controls to sufficiently protect the confidentiality, integrity, and availability of the information and systems that support its mission.[7] For example, the agency did not always (1) protect the boundaries of its networks by ensuring that all incoming traffic was inspected by a firewall; (2) enforce strong policies for identifying and authenticating users by requiring the use of complex passwords; and (3) limit users' access to systems to what was required for them to perform their official duties. The identified weaknesses existed, in part, because the National Archives and Records Administration had not fully implemented key elements of its information security program. As a result, sensitive information, such as records containing personally identifiable information, was at increased and unnecessary risk of unauthorized access, disclosure, modification, or loss. We recommended that it take 224 specific actions to implement elements of its security program and enhance access and other information security controls over its systems. The Archivist of the United States generally concurred with our recommendations, and agreed to provide semiannual updates on the agency's progress to enhance access controls and address the identified weaknesses.

In addition, reviews at the 24 major federal agencies continue to highlight deficiencies in their implementation of information security policies and procedures. In fiscal year 2010, in their performance and accountability reports and annual financial reports, 19 of 24 agencies indicated that inadequate information security controls were either material weaknesses

---

[7]GAO, *Information Security: National Archives and Records Administration Needs to Implement Key Program Elements and Controls*, GAO-11-20 (Washington, D.C.: Oct. 21, 2010).

or significant deficiencies[8] (see fig. 3) for financial reporting purposes. Specifically, 8 agencies identified material weaknesses, increasing from 6 agencies in fiscal year 2009, while 11 reported significant deficiencies, decreasing from 15 agencies in fiscal year 2009.

Figure 3: Number of Major Agencies Reporting Deficiencies in Information Security for Financial Reporting in Fiscal Year 2010

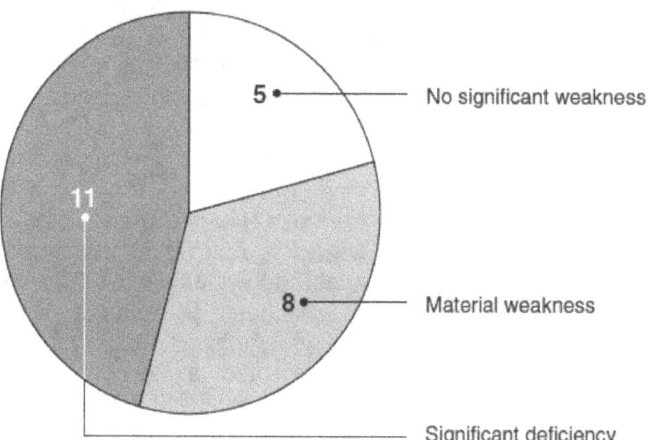

5 — No significant weakness

11

8 — Material weakness

Significant deficiency

Source: GAO analysis of agency performance and accountability reports, annual financial reports, or other financial statement reports for fiscal year 2010.

In fiscal year 2010 annual reports required under 31 U.S.C. § 3512 (commonly referred to as the Federal Managers' Financial Integrity Act of

---

[8]A material weakness is a deficiency, or a combination of deficiencies, in internal control such that there is a reasonable possibility that a material misstatement of the entity's financial statements will not be prevented, or detected and corrected on a timely basis. A significant deficiency is a deficiency, or a combination of deficiencies, in internal control that is less severe than a material weakness, yet important enough to merit attention by those charged with governance. A control deficiency exists when the design or operation of a control does not allow management or employees, in the normal course of performing their assigned functions to prevent, or detect and correct misstatements on a timely basis.

1982),[9] 7 of the 24 agencies identified weaknesses in information security. In addition, 23 of 24 inspectors general cited information security as a "major management challenge" for their agency, reflecting an increase from fiscal year 2009, when 20 of 24 inspectors general cited information security as a challenge.

Weaknesses Noted in All Major Categories of Controls

Our, agency, and inspectors general assessments of information security controls during fiscal year 2010 revealed that most major federal agencies had weaknesses in each of the five major categories of information system controls: (1) access controls, which ensure that only authorized individuals can read, alter, or delete data; (2) configuration management controls, which provide assurance that only authorized software programs are implemented; (3) segregation of duties, which reduces the risk that one individual can independently perform inappropriate actions without detection; (4) continuity of operations planning, which helps avoid significant disruptions in computer-dependent operations; and (5) agencywide information security programs, which provide a framework for ensuring that risks are understood and that effective controls are selected and implemented. All 24 agencies had vulnerabilities in access control, configuration management, and security management. Deficiencies in segregation of duties and contingency planning, while not reported for all of these agencies, were prevalent, as figure 4 demonstrates.

---

[9]The Federal Managers' Financial Integrity Act (FMFIA), Pub. L. No. 97-255, 96 Stat. 814 (Sept. 8, 1982), now codified at 31 U.S.C. § 3512, requires agencies to report annually to the President and Congress on the effectiveness of internal controls and any identified material weaknesses in those controls. Per OMB, for the purposes of FMFIA reporting, a material weakness also encompasses weaknesses found in program operations and compliance with applicable laws and regulations. Material weaknesses for FMFIA reporting are determined by management, whereas material weaknesses reported as part of a financial statement audit are determined by independent auditors.

Figure 4: Information Security Weaknesses at 24 Major Agencies in Fiscal Year 2010

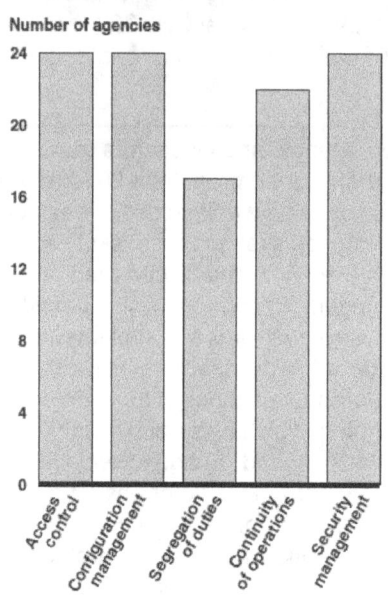

Number of agencies

Information security weakness category

Source: GAO analysis of agency, inspectors general, and GAO reports.

Inadequate Access Controls Placed Information at Risk	Agencies use electronic and physical controls to limit, prevent, or detect inappropriate access to computer resources (data, equipment, and facilities), thereby protecting them from unauthorized use, modification, disclosure, and loss. Access controls involve the six critical elements described in table 1.

Table 1: Critical Elements for Access Control

Element	Description
Boundary Protection	Boundary protection controls logical connectivity into and out of networks and controls connectivity to and from network connected devices. For example, multiple firewalls can be deployed to prevent both outsiders and trusted insiders from gaining unauthorized access to systems, and intrusion detection technologies can be deployed to defend against attacks from the Internet.
User Identification and Authentication	A computer system must be able to identify and authenticate different users so that activities on the system can be linked to specific individuals. When an organization assigns unique user accounts to specific users, the system is able to distinguish one user from another—a process called identification. The system also must establish the validity of a user's claimed identity by requesting some kind of information, such as a password, that is known only by the user—a process known as authentication.
Authorization	Authorization is the process of granting or denying access rights and permissions to a protected resource, such as a network, a system, an application, a function, or a file. For example, operating systems have some built-in authorization features such as permissions for files and folders. Network devices, such as routers, may have access control lists that can be used to authorize users who can access and perform certain actions on the device.
Cryptography	Cryptography underlies many of the mechanisms used to enforce the confidentiality and integrity of critical and sensitive information. Examples of cryptographic services are encryption, authentication, digital signature, and key management. Cryptographic tools help control access to information by making it unintelligible to unauthorized users and by protecting the integrity of transmitted or stored information.
Auditing and Monitoring	To establish individual accountability, monitor compliance with security policies, and investigate security violations, it is necessary to determine what, when, and by whom specific actions have been taken on a system. Agencies do so by implementing software that provides an audit trail, or logs of system activity, that they can use to determine the source of a transaction or attempted transaction and to monitor users' activities.
Physical Security	Physical security controls help protect computer facilities and resources from espionage, sabotage, damage, and theft. Examples of physical security controls include perimeter fencing, surveillance cameras, security guards, locks, and procedures for granting or denying individuals physical access to computing resources. Physical controls also include environmental controls such as smoke detectors, fire alarms, extinguishers, and uninterruptible power supplies. Considerations for perimeter security include controlling vehicular and pedestrian traffic. In addition, visitors' access to sensitive areas is to be managed appropriately.

Source: GAO.

All 24 major federal agencies had access control weaknesses during fiscal year 2010. For example, 18 agencies experienced problems with identifying and authenticating information system users, with at least 7 of these agencies allowing weak authentication practices that could increase vulnerability to unauthorized use of their information systems. Nineteen agencies had weaknesses in controls for authorizing access in such areas as management of inactive accounts and ensuring that only those with a legitimate need had access to sensitive accounts. In addition, 16 agencies did not adequately monitor networks for suspicious activities or report security incidents that had been detected. Without adequate access controls in place, agencies cannot ensure that their information resources are protected from intentional or unintentional harm.

Inconsistent Configuration Management Controls Could Expose Sensitive Information to Unauthorized Use

Configuration management controls ensure that only authorized and fully tested software is placed in operation, software and hardware are updated, information systems are monitored, patches are applied to these systems to protect against known vulnerabilities, and emergency changes are documented and approved. These controls, which limit and monitor access to powerful programs and sensitive files associated with computer operations, are important in providing reasonable assurance that access controls and the operations of systems and networks are not compromised. To protect against known vulnerabilities, effective procedures must be in place, appropriate software installed, and patches updated promptly. Up-to-date patch installation helps mitigate flaws in software code that could be exploited to cause significant damage and enable malicious individuals to read, modify, or delete sensitive information or disrupt operations.

While the 24 major agencies experienced problems with implementing configuration management, no weaknesses were reported in one area: handling emergency changes to system and network configurations. Our and inspectors general assessments revealed weaknesses in other areas, however. Twenty-one agencies had problems with maintaining and adhering to configuration management policies, plans, and procedures, which could jeopardize their ability to manage their systems and networks effectively. Another area where many agencies experienced difficulty was the practice of maintaining current configuration information in a formal baseline.[10] Nineteen agencies had only partially complied with their internal or with federal requirements for maintaining these baselines. In addition, 18 agencies had deficiencies in keeping software updated, such as not adequately managing patch installations. Without a consistent approach to testing, updating, and patching software, agencies increase

---

[10]A formal configuration baseline contains the configuration information designated at a specific time during a product's or component's life. Configuration baselines and approved changes from those baselines constitute the current configuration information. Organizations should maintain a current and comprehensive baseline inventory of hardware, software, and firmware, and it should be routinely validated for accuracy.

their risk of exposing sensitive data to unauthorized and possibly undetected access.

Agencies Did Not Always Adequately Segregate Duties and Responsibilities

Segregation of duties refers to the policies, procedures, and organizational structure that help ensure that one individual cannot independently control all key aspects of a computer-related operation and thereby take unauthorized actions or gain unauthorized access to assets or records. Key steps to achieving proper segregation are ensuring that incompatible duties are separated and employees understand their responsibilities, and controlling personnel activities through formal operating procedures, supervision, and review.

We and agency inspectors general identified 17 agencies that did not adequately segregate duties. Of these agencies, 14 had difficulty ensuring that key duties and responsibilities for authorizing, processing, recording, or reviewing transactions were appropriately separated. For example, 1 agency granted conflicting access to critical resources in its mainframe environment, and another improperly allowed contractors access to security functions. At least 6 of the agencies that did not adequately segregate duties failed to maintain sufficient control over personnel procedures, supervision, and review. At 1 agency, there was no effective way to identify how many contractors had access to and privileges within the network, and at least 3 agencies allowed individuals to inappropriately use accounts with elevated privileges or assume conflicting roles. Without adequate segregation of duties, agencies increase the risk that erroneous or fraudulent actions will occur, improper program changes will be implemented, and computer resources will be damaged or destroyed.

Continuity of Operations Plans Lacked Important Details

In the event of an act of nature, fire, accident, sabotage, or other disruption, an essential element in preparing for the loss of operational capabilities is having an up-to-date, detailed, and fully tested continuity of operations plan. This plan should cover all key functions, including assessing an agency's information technology and identifying resources, minimizing potential damage and interruption, developing and documenting the plan, and testing it and making necessary adjustments. If continuity of operations controls are faulty, even relatively minor interruptions can result in lost or incorrectly processed data, which can lead to financial losses, expensive recovery efforts, and inaccurate or incomplete mission-critical information.

Our and agency inspectors general fiscal year 2010 reports show that 22 federal agencies had shortcomings in their plans for continuity of operations. Developing and implementing a comprehensive plan presented difficulties for at least 13 agencies for varying reasons. For example, 1 agency did not include key elements in some contingency plans or testing reports, such as identification of alternate processing facilities, restoration procedures, and data-sensitivity handling procedures, and officials at another agency were confused about their responsibilities for contingency and disaster recovery planning for certain classified systems. Additionally, tests of existing plans proved to be inadequate for at least 11 agencies. Until agencies address identified weaknesses in their continuity of operations plans and tests of these plans, they may not be able to recover systems in a successful and timely manner when service disruptions occur.

Agencywide Security Programs Were Not Fully Implemented

An underlying cause for information security weaknesses identified at federal agencies is that they have not yet fully or effectively implemented an agencywide information security program. An agencywide security program, as required by FISMA, provides a framework for assessing and managing risk, including developing and implementing security policies and procedures, conducting security awareness training, monitoring the adequacy of the entity's computer-related controls through security tests and evaluations, and implementing remedial actions as appropriate. Without a well-designed program, security controls may be inadequate; responsibilities may be unclear, misunderstood, and improperly implemented; and controls may be inconsistently applied. Such conditions may lead to insufficient protection of sensitive or critical resources.

Of the 24 major agencies, none had fully or effectively implemented an agencywide information security program. To illustrate, 18 had shortcomings in the documentation of their security management programs, which establishes the framework and activities for assessing risk, developing and implementing effective security procedures, and monitoring the effectiveness of these procedures. In another example, 18 agencies did not adequately implement remedial actions to correct known vulnerabilities.

Until agencies fully resolve identified deficiencies in their agencywide information security programs, the federal government will continue to face significant challenges in protecting its information systems and networks. We continue to identify information security as a governmentwide high-risk issue in our biennial reports to Congress, most recently in February 2011.[11] Full and effective implementation of agencywide information security programs is necessary to ensure that federal data and systems will be adequately safeguarded to prevent disruption, unauthorized use, disclosure, and modification.

Actions Under Way, but More Work Necessary for Implementing FISMA Requirements

OMB, executive branch agencies, and NIST have taken actions intended to improve the implementation of their FISMA-related security requirements, but much work remains. Beginning in fiscal year 2009, OMB instituted the use of a new online tool for agencies to report their information security posture on a recurring basis and, in fiscal year 2010, provided them with new and revised metrics for reporting such information. However, not all the metrics used to measure performance included performance targets. While agencies reported performance using these new and revised metrics, inspectors general continued to identify weaknesses in the processes agencies used to implement the requirements.

OMB Has Taken Several Actions Aimed at Improving Federal Information Security but Continued Progress Needed

As previously discussed, FISMA requires OMB to develop and oversee the implementation of policies, standards, and guidelines on information security at executive branch agencies and to annually report on agency compliance with FISMA to Congress no later than March 1 of each year. In fulfilling these and other requirements, OMB has taken a number of actions intended to meet its FISMA responsibilities and improve federal information security. These include:

- *Launching a new security reporting tool—Cyberscope*. In fiscal year 2010, OMB mandated that agencies use Cyberscope for submitting their information security data to OMB. Cyberscope is an interactive data collection tool that has the capability to receive data feeds on a recurring basis to assess the security posture of a federal agency's information infrastructure. According to OMB, this tool will allow agencies to report security data on a more frequent basis. Beginning in 2011, agencies are required to report data on a monthly basis, rather than the previous quarterly basis.

---

[11]GAO, *High-Risk Series: An Update*, GAO-11-278 (Washington, D.C.: February 2011).

- *Developing new security metrics.* In fiscal year 2010, OMB convened a joint task force[12] that developed new security performance metrics that are intended to encourage agencies to focus on risk and improve information security. We previously recommended that OMB develop additional measures of effectiveness.[13] According to OMB, the new security metrics are intended to provide "outcome-focused" metrics for federal agencies to assess the implementation of security capabilities, measure their effectiveness, and ascertain their impact on risk levels. The revised metrics included reporting on:

  - Boundary protection—to report information on the status of agencies' implementation of the Trusted Internet Connections initiative,[14] such as the percentage of external connections or network capacity passing through a trusted Internet connection; or to report on agencies' deployment of operational Einstein 2 sensors,[15] such as the percentage of trusted Internet connections with operational Einstein 2 deployments.

  - Remote access and telework—to report information on the methods allowed to remotely connect to agency network resources.

---

[12]Participants in the task force were the federal Chief Information Officers Council, the Council of Inspectors General on Integrity and Efficiency, NIST, DHS, the Information Security and Privacy Advisory Board, and the President's Cybersecurity Coordinator. In addition, GAO was an observer to this task force.

[13]GAO, *Information Security: Concerted Effort Needed to Improve Federal Performance Measures*, GAO-09-617 (Washington, D.C.: Sept. 14, 2009).

[14]The Trusted Internet Connections initiative is intended to improve security by reducing the number of, and strengthening the security over, the access points through which external network connections can be made and by providing centralized monitoring at a select group of access providers.

[15]US-CERT developed the Einstein system to detect and identify cybersecurity threats and suspicious activity in near-real time.

- Identity and access management—to report on the extent to which agencies have issued and implemented personal identity verification cards in accordance with Homeland Security Presidential Directive 12.[16]

- Data protection—to report agencies' use of encryption on portable computers, such as laptops.

OMB has also acted to assign the operational aspects of several of its FISMA-related responsibilities to DHS. In July 2010, the Director of OMB and the Cybersecurity Coordinator[17] issued a joint memorandum[18] stating that DHS will exercise primary responsibility within the executive branch for the operational aspects of federal agency cybersecurity with respect to federal information systems that fall within the scope of FISMA. In carrying out this responsibility and the accompanying activities, DHS is to be subject to general OMB oversight in accordance with the provisions of FISMA. According to the memorandum, DHS responsibilities include but are not limited to

- overseeing the governmentwide and agency-specific implementation of and reporting on cybersecurity policies and guidance;

- overseeing and assisting governmentwide and agency-specific efforts to provide adequate, risk-based, and cost-effective cybersecurity;

- overseeing the agencies' compliance with FISMA and developing analyses for OMB to assist in the development of the FISMA annual report;

---

[16] HSPD-12, issued in August 2004, directed the establishment of a mandatory, governmentwide standard for secure and reliable forms of identification for federal government employees and contractors that access government-controlled facilities and information systems.

[17] In December 2009, a Special Assistant to the President and Cybersecurity Coordinator, referred as the Cybersecurity Coordinator, was appointed with responsbility for addressing the recommendations made in the Cyberspace Policy Review, including coordinating interagency cybersecurity policies and strategies and developing a comprehensive national strategy to secure the nation's digital infrastructure.

[18] OMB, Memorandum M-10-28, *Clarifying Cybersecurity Responsibilities and Activities of the Executive Office of the President and the Department of Homeland Security* (Washington, D.C.: July 6, 2010).

- overseeing the agencies' cybersecurity operations and incident response and providing appropriate assistance; and

- reviewing the agencies' cybersecurity programs annually.

In fiscal year 2011, DHS, as part of implementing its new operational information security responsibilities, held meetings with chief information officers and chief information security officers from the 24 major federal agencies. According to DHS officials, the meetings were aimed at allowing agency officials to discuss specific challenges they faced in addressing threats and vulnerabilities and assisting DHS with determining the capabilities needed to address persistent issues. Additionally, DHS launched "CyberStat" review sessions in January 2011 with the purpose of ensuring accountability and assisting the agencies in driving progress with key strategic enterprise cybersecurity capabilities. Data used in CyberStat sessions are based on information provided by agencies through CyberScope. According to both OMB and DHS officials, as of July 2011, DHS has held CyberStat sessions with seven agencies discussing various topics including continuous monitoring.

In addition, OMB satisfied its FISMA requirement to report to the Congress no later than March 1, 2011, on agency compliance with FISMA. OMB transmitted its fiscal year 2010 report and highlighted achievements across the federal government that included, among others, a shift from periodic security reviews to automated mechanisms for continuously monitoring agency security controls, the use of NIST's Risk Management Framework concepts,[19] and the approval of the National Initiative for Cyber Education, which is intended to improve cybersecurity education through the establishment of education and training programs. The report also references efforts taken by the Office of Personnel Management to develop a cybersecurity competency model and review human resource strategies to help hire and retain cybersecurity experts to meet existing and future federal workforce needs. We have ongoing work in the area of cybersecurity human capital workforce planning activities.

---

[19]NIST, *Guide for Applying the Risk Management Framework to Federal Information Systems: A Security Life Cycle Approach, Special Publication 800-37*, Revision 1, (Gaithersburg, Md., February 2010).

OMB Improved Reporting, but Did Not Always Include Targets to Measure Performance

For fiscal year 2010, OMB enhanced the FISMA reporting process. FISMA requires that OMB report on agencies' compliance with the act's requirements. Each year, OMB provides instructions to federal agencies and their inspectors general for preparing their FISMA reports and then summarizes the information provided by the agencies and their inspectors general in its report to Congress. In its annual information security reporting instructions to agencies and their inspectors general, OMB expanded the number and type of security control areas covered under the reporting process. For the first time, OMB required agencies to provide information on their use of automated tools to manage, for example, information technology configurations and vulnerabilities. In addition, agencies were to provide information with regard to, among other things, security awareness training, configuration management, and incident management.

We had previously recommended that OMB expand inspectors general reporting to address additional security program areas.[20] Accordingly, for fiscal year 2010, OMB's reporting instructions also identified additional areas for which inspectors general were to assess and report on agency performance; such areas included identity management and continuous monitoring.

Even with these changes, continued improvements are needed. Specifically, as we previously reported, one attribute of a metric is that it should be meaningful.[21] A meaningful metric should be clear, address organizational priorities, and have performance targets. OMB's fiscal year 2010 reporting instructions included 31 metrics for chief information officers. While most chief information officer metrics were clearly defined and reflected agency priorities, all but one of the metrics did not include performance targets that would allow agencies to track progress over time. For example, one of the measures asks agencies to provide the mean time for incident detection, remediation, and recovery. While this defined metric addresses an organizational priority, it does not provide a target or threshold to monitor progress over time.

---

[20]GAO, *Information Security: Agencies Continue to Report Progress, but Need to Mitigate Persistent Weaknesses*, GAO-09-546 (Washington, D.C.: July 17, 2009).

[21]GAO-09-617.

Inspectors general were also asked to comment on various program areas, but the measures provided do not distinguish performance targets to determine levels of effective implementation. To illustrate, inspectors general are asked to report whether their agency's security authorization program includes "categorizes information systems" as an "attribute" of the program. However, there is no specific target or measure to determine whether this would mean that a specific portion of systems had been properly categorized (e.g., all or half), or just systems in the inspectors general review.

According to OMB officials, targets were not included since targets are set based on the Administration's top cyber security priorities or by NIST standards and guidance. For example, in February 2011, OMB and DHS set several targets for implementing various Homeland Security Presidential Directive 12 requirements in their memorandum to federal agencies. While targets may be provided in various memorandums and guidance, agencies may still be unaware of the thresholds that are to be met as part of their annual report requirements. Further, without specific targets listed in annual reporting instructions and identified in annual FISMA reports, federal agencies and the Congress may not be able to properly gauge performance.

Weaknesses in Agencies' Security Practices Continue as Agencies Report Performance Using New Measures

While agencies reported on their information security programs using new and revised measures, they continued to have weaknesses in implementing security practices. In addition to categories used in fiscal year 2009 such as security awareness and specialized training, agencies also reported on their capability to automate the management of information system asset configurations and vulnerabilities. Inspectors general also reported agencies' program performance using new measures for categories such as continuous monitoring, among others, and identified weaknesses in agencies programs' both in new categories and those used in prior years.

Agencies Provided Awareness and Specialized Training, but Inspectors General Highlighted Implementation Weaknesses

FISMA requires agencies to provide security awareness training to personnel, including contractors and other users of information systems that support agency operations and assets. This training should explain information security risks associated with their activities and their responsibilities in complying with agency policies and procedures designed to reduce these risks. In addition, agencies are required to provide appropriate information security training to personnel who have significant security responsibilities. For fiscal year 2010, OMB required agencies to report, among other things, (1) the number of agency users with log-in privileges who had been given security awareness training annually and (2) the number of agency users with significant security responsibilities who had been given specialized, role-based, security training annually.

In fiscal year 2010, the 24 major agencies reported that 92 percent of users with log-in privileges had been given annual security awareness training, and that 88 percent of users with significant security responsibilities had received specialized training. However, while most of the major agencies reported a high percentage of users receiving awareness training, the number of agencies reporting a high percentage of users receiving specialized training was about half that number (see fig. 5).

Figure 5: Percentage of Users Trained at 24 Major Agencies in Fiscal Year 2010

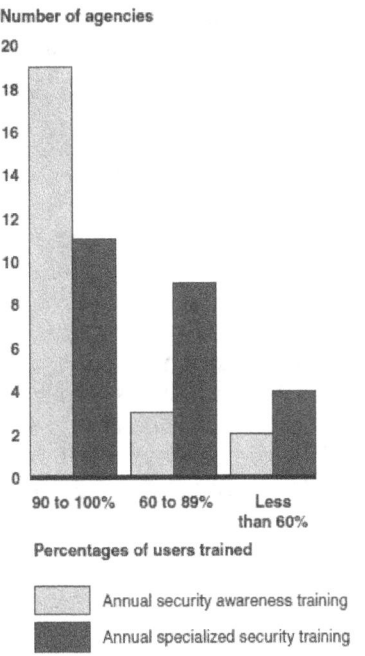

Number of agencies

Percentages of users trained

☐ Annual security awareness training
■ Annual specialized security training

Source: GAO analysis of agency fiscal year 2010 data.

Even with the high overall percentages reported for users receiving training, inspectors general continued to identify weaknesses in their agency's training program. Specifically, inspectors general for 17 of 24 major agencies cited weaknesses in their agency's training programs. For example, 5 inspectors general reported that less than 90 percent of employees with log-in privileges had attended security awareness training in the last year. In addition, 11 inspectors general reported that less than 90 percent of employees, contractors, and other users with significant security responsibilities had attended specialized training in the past year. Inspectors general for 11 agencies also reported that identification and tracking of those with significant security responsibilities were not adequate. As a result, these agencies have less assurance that users are aware of the information security risks and their responsibilities for reducing such risks.

Agencies Reported New Capabilities, but Inspectors General Reported Configuration Management Weaknesses

FISMA requires each agency to have policies and procedures that ensure compliance with minimally acceptable system configuration requirements, as determined by the agency. In fiscal year 2010 reporting, for the first time, OMB required agencies to provide an estimated number of IT assets where an automated capability[22] provides visibility into system configuration information and vulnerabilities. In addition, inspectors general were also requested to report on their agency's configuration management program.

Agencies varied in automated capabilities for monitoring their IT configurations and vulnerabilities. Specifically, 2 agencies reported having an automated management system that allowed them to monitor the configurations for 90 to 100 percent of their assets; 8 reported being able to monitor configurations for 60 to 89 percent of their assets; and 14 reported being able to monitor less than 60 percent of their assets. Similarly, automated monitoring for vulnerabilities varied among agencies. Four agencies were able to monitor 90 to 100 percent of their assets for vulnerabilities; 10 reported being able to monitor 60 to 89 percent of their assets for vulnerabilities; and 10 reported being able to monitor less than 60 percent of their assets for vulnerabilities (see fig. 6).

[22]OMB describes its goal of IT asset management capability as having 100 percent of agency assets under an automated asset management system that captures the necessary data (i.e., configuration and vulnerabilities) about each asset and can provide it within a short period of time.

Figure 6: Automated Management Capabilities Reported by 24 Major Agencies in Fiscal Year 2010

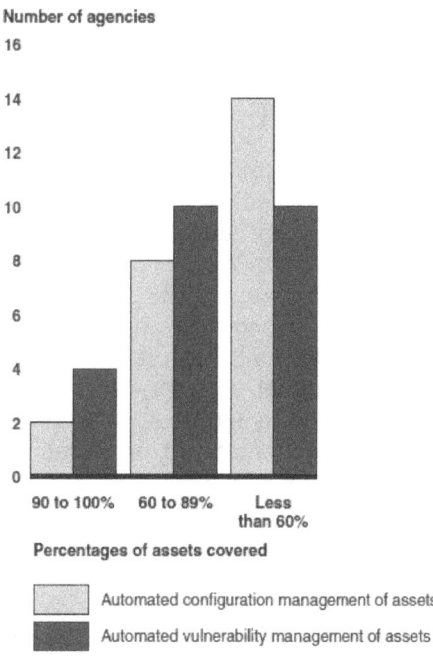

Number of agencies

Percentages of assets covered

☐ Automated configuration management of assets
■ Automated vulnerability management of assets

Source: GAO analysis of agency fiscal year 2010 data.

While agencies reported on their capabilities, inspectors general reported configuration management weaknesses. For example, 18 of 24 inspectors general reported that their agency had weaknesses in its configuration management programs, and 16 indicated their agency's patch management processes for mitigating software flaws were not fully developed.[23] If agencies do not properly implement configuration management practices, systems may not be configured adequately to protect against vulnerabilities, which could increase the risk of compromise to those systems.

---

[23]Patch management is the systematic notification, identification, deployment, installation, and verification of operating system and application software code revisions. These revisions are known as patches, hot fixes, and service packs.

Controls Were Not Always Effectively Tested and Evaluated through Continuous Monitoring Activities

FISMA requires that federal agencies periodically test and evaluate the effectiveness of their information security policies, procedures, and practices as part of implementing an agencywide security program. This testing is to be performed with a frequency depending on risk, but no less than annually, and includes testing management, operational, and technical controls for every system identified in the agency's required inventory of major systems.

In its fiscal year 2010 reporting instructions, OMB informed agencies that they could meet their testing requirement by drawing upon security control assessment results that include, but are not limited to, continuous monitoring activities. According to NIST, continuous monitoring of security controls is a key activity of risk management. It allows an organization to maintain an ongoing awareness of information security, vulnerabilities, and threats that supports its organizational risk management decisions. The objectives are to (1) conduct ongoing monitoring of the security of an organization's networks, information, and systems, and (2) respond by accepting, transferring, or mitigating risk as situations change. As part of its fiscal year 2010 reporting instructions, OMB requested inspectors general to report whether agencies had established a continuous monitoring program.

Most of the agencies had not fully implemented their programs for continuous monitoring of security controls. We and inspectors general identified weaknesses in 17 of 24 agencies' fiscal year 2010 efforts for continuous monitoring.[24] For example, we reported that while the Department of State is recognized as a leader in federal efforts to develop and implement a continuous risk monitoring capability, it did not have a documented continuous monitoring strategy in place, among other weaknesses. In addition, 2 inspectors general also reported that their respective agencies had not established a continuous monitoring program. While 15 inspectors general reported that their agencies had programs in place, all cited weaknesses in their agency's programs. These weaknesses included, for example, that continuous monitoring procedures were not fully developed or consistently implemented at 11 agencies. In another example, 10 inspectors general cited weaknesses in ongoing assessments of selected security controls. Similarly, inspectors

---

[24]GAO, *Information Security: State Has Taken Steps to Implement a Continuous Monitoring Application, but Key Challenges Remain*, GAO-11-149 (Washington, D.C.: July 8, 2011).

general at 9 agencies reported that information, such as status reports covering continuous monitoring results, was not provided to key officials. As a result, agencies may not have reasonable assurance that controls have been implemented correctly, are operating as intended, and are producing the desired outcome with respect to meeting the security requirements of the agency.

Agencies Did Not Always Ensure that Weaknesses Were Remediated

FISMA requires that agencies' information security programs include a process for planning, implementing, evaluating, and documenting remedial actions to address any deficiencies in the information security policies, procedures, and practices of the agency. OMB emphasized that these remedial action plans—known as Plans of Action and Milestones (POA&M)—should include all security weaknesses found during any other review done by, for, or on behalf of the agency and be the authoritative agencywide management tool, inclusive of all evaluations. OMB also requested that inspectors general report on whether agencies have established and maintained a POA&M program.

Although 8 inspectors general did not identify deficiencies with their agency's remediation program, 16 reported that, while their agency had established and maintained a POA&M program, weaknesses were not always effectively managed. For example, 12 inspectors general reported that POA&Ms did not include all known security weaknesses, 10 reported that the plans were not updated in a timely manner, and 10 reported that costs of remediation efforts were not identified. Without a sound remediation process, agencies cannot be assured that information security weaknesses are being corrected and managed.

Agencies Did Not Always Manage Incidents

FISMA requires that agency security programs include procedures for detecting, reporting, and responding to security incidents. For fiscal year 2010 reporting, OMB required agencies to report the percentages of incidents detected by their network or security operations centers (NOC/SOC) and the mean time-to-incident detection, remediation, and recovery for their networks.

Agencies varied widely in their performance of these measures. To illustrate, 10 agencies reported that their NOC/SOC detected 90-100 percent of incidents, 8 reported 50-89 percent, and 6 reported less than 50 percent (see fig. 7).

Figure 7: Percentage of Incidents Detected by Federal Agencies' NOC/SOC in Fiscal Year 2010

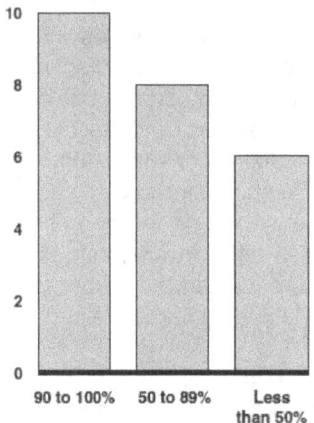

Number of agencies

Percentages of incidents detected

Source: GAO analysis of agency fiscal year 2010 data.

Agencies also differed widely in the average time it took them to recover from an incident. To illustrate, 10 agencies reported average incident recovery times that were less than 1 hour, while 4 reported recovery times that exceeded 250 hours, with one reporting an average time that exceeded 900 hours.

Inspectors general for nine agencies highlighted weaknesses in incident response and reporting. Of the nine inspectors general identifying weaknesses, eight reported that incident monitoring and detection coverage was insufficient; seven reported that incident procedures were not fully developed, sufficiently detailed, or consistently implemented; and seven reported that incidents were not identified in a timely manner. Ineffective incident management controls may reduce agencies' ability to discover, respond to, or prevent future incidents or exploits.

Contingency Planning Was Not Adequate

FISMA requires that agencywide information security programs include plans and procedures to ensure continuity of operations for information systems that support the operations and assets of the agency. For fiscal year 2010 reporting, OMB no longer requested agencies to report the number of tested contingency plans, but requested the inspectors general to report on their agency's efforts to establish a program for contingency planning.

Inspectors general for 16 agencies highlighted weaknesses in their agency's program for contingency planning. For example, 11 of the 16 inspectors general highlighting weaknesses reported that contingency planning procedures were not fully developed or consistently implemented. Similarly, inspectors general for 10 agencies reported that system contingency plans were missing key information, and 8 reported that contingency plans were not tested. If contingency plans are not completed and tested, agencies have less assurance that they can appropriately recover key systems in a timely manner should disruptions occur.

Inventories Increased Slightly, but May Not Accurately Reflect the Number of Systems

FISMA requires agencies to maintain and update annually an inventory of major information systems (including major national security systems) operated by the agency or under its control, which includes an identification of the interfaces between each system and all other systems or networks, including those not operated by or under the control of the agency. The Federal Information Processing Standards Publication 199, Standards for Security Categorization of Federal Information and Information Systems, defines three impact levels where the loss of confidentiality, integrity, or availability could be expected to have a limited adverse effect (low), a serious adverse effect (moderate), or a severe or catastrophic adverse effect (high) on organizational operations, organizational assets, or individuals.

For fiscal year 2010, OMB required agencies to report the number of agency and contractor systems by impact levels. Major agencies reported a total of 11,310 systems, composed of 9,818 agency and 1,492 contractor systems, as shown by impact level in table 2. This represents a slight increase in the total number of systems from fiscal year 2009, with the number of agency systems increasing and the number of contractor systems decreasing.

Table 2: Total Number of Agency and Contractor Systems in Fiscal Years 2009 and 2010 by Impact Level

Impact level	Agency		Contractor		Total	
	FY09	FY10	FY09	FY10	FY09	FY10
High	1,123	1,179	146	117	1,269	1,296
Moderate	4,138	4,734	598	675	4,736	5,409
Low	3,926	3,619	375	311	4,301	3,930
Not categorized	213	286	570	389	783	675
Total	9,400	9,818	1,689	1,492	11,089	11,310

Source: GAO analysis of agency fiscal years 2009 and 2010 data.

Although not requested to report on agencies' entire inventory in fiscal year 2010, 12 inspectors general highlighted weaknesses in the accuracy of their agency's inventory. For example, one inspector general reported that its agency's inventory was not reconciled and that two systems used to track the inventory were not consistent with each other. Another inspector general reported that systems identified in fiscal year 2009 should have been designated as contractor systems for fiscal year 2010, but the agency had not corrected its designations for all the identified systems. Without a complete and accurate inventory, an agency has less assurance that it is effectively maintaining and securing its systems since all assets may not be identified correctly.

Agencies Reported High Percentages of Security Authorizations, but Inspectors General Identified Weaknesses in the Process

OMB has continued to emphasize its long-standing policy of requiring a management official to formally authorize an information system to process information and accept the risk associated with its operation based on an evaluation of the system's security controls. However, according to OMB, rather than enforcing a static, 3-year reauthorization process,[25] it expects agencies to conduct ongoing authorizations of information systems through a risk management process that includes continuous monitoring.

In addition, agencies are required to follow the guidance in NIST Special Publication 800-37, Revision 1, which emphasizes, among other things, ongoing information system authorizations through continuous monitoring

---

[25]OMB reported that the term certification and accreditation, which has been used to describe the 3-year reauthorization process, was eliminated with the release of NIST Special Publication 800-37 in February 2010.

processes. For fiscal year 2010, OMB required agencies to report the number of systems receiving security authorizations.[26] OMB also requested that inspectors general report on their agency's security authorization processes.

Agencies reported that 92 percent of all their systems received authorization for fiscal year 2010. Specifically, agencies reported security authorizations of 92 percent for high-impact systems, 93 percent for moderate-impact systems, 92 percent for low-impact systems, and 87 percent for those not categorized.

While most systems received a security authorization, inspectors general reported deficiencies in the quality of the security authorization process at their agencies. Specifically, 11 of 24 inspectors general identified weaknesses in their agency's authorization processes. To illustrate, 8 inspectors general reported that security authorization procedures were not fully developed, sufficiently detailed, or consistently implemented, and 7 reported that minimum baseline security controls were not adequately applied to information systems. Additionally, 6 reported that risk assessments were not adequately conducted, 8 reported that security plans did not adequately identify security requirements, and 9 reported that the process to assess security control effectiveness was inadequate. These weaknesses could reduce agencies' assurance that risks are identified and mitigated before systems are placed into operation.

Agencies Reported Efforts to Implement Privacy Requirements

In its FISMA reporting instructions for fiscal year 2009,[27] OMB informed agencies that it was using the FISMA reporting vehicle to address privacy reporting requirements and to reduce the reporting burden on the agencies. For fiscal year 2010, OMB required the senior agency official for privacy at each agency to report privacy program performance using similar questions to those from fiscal year 2009. Among other questions,

---

[26]NIST Special Publication 800-37, Revision 1, defines a security authorization as the official management decision given by a senior organization official to authorize operation of an information system and to explicitly accept the risk to organization operations and assets, individuals, other organizations, and the nation based on the implementation of an agreed-upon set of security controls.

[27]OMB, Memorandum M-09-29, *FY2009 Reporting Instructions for the Federal Information Security Management Act and Agency Privacy Management* (Washington, D.C.: Aug. 20, 2009).

agencies were required to report information about the implementation of their privacy policies and training.

For fiscal year 2010 reporting, agencies reported that they implemented privacy requirements. For example, the 24 major agencies all reported having policies in place to ensure personnel with access to federal data were generally familiar with information privacy laws, regulations, and policies. In addition, all 24 reported having a program for job-specific and information privacy training, and 17 reported using technologies that enable continuous auditing of compliance with privacy policies and practices.

Weaknesses Identified in Agency Oversight of Contractors

FISMA's information security program requirements also apply to information systems used or operated by a contractor of an agency or other agency on behalf of an agency. Activities performed by contractors or third-party services should be secure since contractors providing systems and services or other users with privileged access to agency systems, applications, and data can introduce risks to information and systems. For fiscal year 2010, OMB revised its reporting guidance to request that inspectors general report whether agencies had established and maintained a program to oversee systems operated on their behalf by contractors or other entities.

Inspectors general for 18 agencies identified weaknesses in agency programs for overseeing contractor operations. For example, inspectors general for 2 agencies revealed that their agency did not have a program in place, and the remaining 16 identified weaknesses in their agency's program. Illustrative examples included 10 inspectors general reporting that their agency had not fully developed or consistently implemented policies and procedures to oversee systems operated on the agency's behalf by contractors or other entities. Eight inspectors general also reported that systems owned or operated by contractors and entities did not meet OMB and NIST FISMA requirements. Without effective programs for oversight of contractors, agencies may not be aware of risks that could place federal information and operations at risk.

NIST Continues to Fulfill Its FISMA Requirements

NIST has produced several information security standards and guidelines required by FISMA under its two-phase FISMA Implementation Project. The first phase focuses on the development of security standards (federal information processing standards) and guidance (Special Publications in the 800 series) necessary for effectively implementing provisions of the act. At this time, phase I of the FISMA Implementation Project is nearing completion, and NIST has finalized six special publications and two standards for information security. Future plans for this phase include updating draft publications related to risk management and completing a systems and security engineering guideline and application security guideline.

The second phase of the FISMA Implementation Project is focused on providing information system implementation and assessment reference materials for building common understanding in applying the NIST suite of publications supporting the Risk Management Framework. Phase II initiatives include, among others, the development of training courses; tools supporting implementation and assessment of SP 800-53-based security controls; and the development of an information security assessment credentialing program for public and private sector organizations that provide these services for federal agencies.

Conclusions

Persistent governmentwide weaknesses in information security controls threaten the confidentiality, integrity, and availability of the information and information systems supporting the operations and assets of federal agencies. Inadequacies exist in access controls, which include identification and authentication, authorization, cryptography, audit and monitoring, boundary protection, and physical security. Weaknesses also exist in other controls such as configuration management, segregation of duties, and continuity of operations. These shortcomings leave federal agencies vulnerable to external as well as internal threats. As long as agencies have not fully and effectively implemented their information security programs, including addressing the hundreds of recommendations that we and inspectors general have made, federal systems will remain at increased risk of attack or compromise.

The new reporting tool and metrics issued by OMB might improve the visibility of agencies' future implementation of the act. The FISMA reporting process and new performance measures are intended to improve agencies' information security programs, but the measures did not usually include performance targets. NIST, the inspectors general, and OMB have all taken actions toward fulfilling their FISMA requirements. However, deficiencies continued to be identified in agencies' programs, such as training for personnel with significant responsibilities, remediation of security weaknesses, and resolving incidents in a timely manner. Weaknesses were also identified in new OMB-defined program categories, such as identity management and continuous monitoring. As such, information that agencies reported may not accurately reflect their implementation of required information security policies and procedures. Until hundreds of recommendations made by us and inspectors general are implemented and program weaknesses are corrected, agencies will continue to face challenges in securing their information and information systems.

Recommendation for Executive Action

We recommend that the Director of the Office of Management and Budget take the following action:

- Incorporate performance targets for metrics in annual FISMA reporting guidance to agencies and inspectors general.

Agency Comments and Our Evaluation

We provided a draft of this report to OMB and DHS for their review. We received e-mail comments from an OMB representative. In response to our recommendation, OMB stated that since, unlike in previous years, OMB and DHS now issue separate memoranda regarding FISMA reporting guidance, it is more appropriate for the performance targets to be included in DHS's memorandum since that is where the metrics are listed. We agree that including the performance targets in the metrics issued by DHS would meet the intent of our recommendation.

In written comments, reproduced in appendix III, DHS's Director of the Departmental GAO/OIG Liaison Office, noted that he was pleased with GAO's acknowledgement of efforts made by DHS to improve the cybersecurity posture of federal agencies. DHS also provided technical comments, which we have incorporated into this report as appropriate. We also provided a draft of this report to the seven other agencies included in our review (the Departments of Health and Human Services, the Interior, Justice, and Veterans Affairs; the National Institute of Standards and Technology; the Office of Personnel Management; and the U.S. Agency for International Development). All seven responded that they did not have any comments.

We are sending copies of this report to the Director of the Office of Management and Budget and other interested parties. In addition, this report will be available at no charge on the GAO website at http://www.gao.gov.

If you have any questions regarding this report, please contact me at (202) 512-6244 or wilshuseng@gao.gov. Contact points for our Offices of Congressional Relations and Public Affairs may be found on the last page of this report. Key contributors to this report are listed in appendix III.

Gregory C. Wilshusen
Director, Information Security Issues

Appendix I: Objectives, Scope, and Methodology

In accordance with the Federal Information Security Management Act of 2002[1] (FISMA) requirement that the Comptroller General report periodically to the Congress, our objectives were to evaluate (1) the adequacy and effectiveness of agencies' information security policies and practices and (2) federal agencies' implementation of FISMA requirements.

To assess the adequacy and effectiveness of agencies' information security policies and practices, we analyzed our related reports issued from July 2009 through March 2011. We also reviewed and analyzed the information security work and products of the Offices of Inspector General at the 24 major federal agencies covered by the Chief Financial Officers Act for fiscal years 2009 and 2010. Further, we reviewed and summarized weaknesses identified in our reports and those of inspectors general using the five major categories of information security general controls identified in our Federal Information System Controls Audit Manual: (1) access controls, (2) configuration management controls, (3) segregation of duties, (4) continuity of operations planning, and (5) agencywide information security programs.[2] Further, we reviewed and analyzed data on information security in federal agencies' performance and accountability and financial reports for fiscal year 2010.

To assess the implementation of FISMA requirements, we reviewed and analyzed the provisions of the act and the FISMA data submissions for 24 major federal agencies for fiscal years 2009 and 2010. In addition, we reviewed the mandated annual FISMA reports from the Office of Management and Budget and the National Institute of Standards and Technology, as well as the Department of Homeland Security's U.S. Computer Emergency Readiness Team report of security incidents for fiscal year 2010. We also examined the Office of Management and Budget's reporting instructions and other guidance related to FISMA.

To assess the reliability of the FISMA data, we selected 6 agencies to gain an understanding of the quality of processes in place to produce both chief information officer and inspectors general FISMA reports. To select these agencies, we sorted the 24 major agencies from highest to

---

[1]Pub. L. No. 107-347, Title III, 116 Stat. 2899, 2946 (Dec. 17, 2002).

[2]GAO, *Federal Information System Controls Audit Manual*, GAO-09-232G (Washington, D.C.: February 2009).

lowest using the total number of systems the agencies reported in fiscal year 2009; separated them into even categories of large, medium, and small agencies; then selected the median 2 agencies from each category. These agencies were: the United States Agency for International Development, the Department of the Interior, the Office of Personnel Management, the Department of Justice, the Department of Veterans Affairs, and the Department of Health and Human Services.

We conducted interviews and performed limited testing with the inspectors general and agency officials from the selected agencies to determine the reliability of FISMA data submissions for 24 major federal agencies for fiscal years 2009 and 2010. We also accessed the CyberScope system to gain an understanding of the data, related internal controls, missing data, outliers, and obvious errors and reviewed supporting documentation that agencies provided to corroborate information provided in their responses. As appropriate, we interviewed officials from the Office of Management and Budget, the Department of Commerce's National Institute for Standards and Technology, and the Department of Homeland Security. We did not evaluate the implementation of the Department of Homeland Security's FISMA-related responsibilities assigned to it by the Office of Management and Budget. Based on this assessment, we determined that the data were sufficiently reliable for our work.

We conducted this performance audit from September 2010 to October 2011 in accordance with generally accepted government auditing standards. Those standards require that we plan and perform the audit to obtain sufficient, appropriate evidence to provide a reasonable basis for our findings and conclusions based on our audit objectives. We believe that the evidence obtained provides a reasonable basis for our findings and conclusions based on our audit objectives.

Appendix II: FISMA Responsibilities

Responsibilities of the Office of Management and Budget

FISMA states that the Director of the Office of Management and Budget (OMB) shall oversee agency information security policies and practices, including:

- developing and overseeing the implementation of policies, principles, standards, and guidelines on information security;

- requiring agencies to identify and provide information security protections commensurate with risk and magnitude of the harm resulting from the unauthorized access, use, disclosure, disruption, modification, or destruction of information collected or maintained by or on behalf of an agency, or information systems used or operated by an agency, or by a contractor of an agency, or other organization on behalf of an agency;

- overseeing agency compliance with FISMA; and

- reviewing at least annually and approving or disapproving, agency information security programs.

FISMA also requires OMB to report to Congress no later than March 1 of each year on agency compliance with the requirements of the act.

Agency Responsibilities

FISMA requires each agency, including agencies with national security systems, to develop, document, and implement an agencywide information security program to provide security for the information and information systems that support the operations and assets of the agency, including those provided or managed by another agency, contractor, or other source.

Specifically, FISMA requires information security programs to include, among other things:

- periodic assessments of the risk and magnitude of harm that could result from the unauthorized access, use, disclosure, disruption, modification, or destruction of information or information systems;

- risk-based policies and procedures that cost-effectively reduce information security risks to an acceptable level and ensure that information security is addressed throughout the life cycle of each information system;

- subordinate plans for providing adequate information security for networks, facilities, and systems or groups of information systems, as appropriate;

- security awareness training for agency personnel, including contractors and other users of information systems that support the operations and assets of the agency;

- periodic testing and evaluation of the effectiveness of information security policies, procedures, and practices, performed with a frequency depending on risk, but no less than annually, and that includes testing of management, operational, and technical controls for every system identified in the agency's required inventory of major information systems;

- a process for planning, implementing, evaluating, and documenting remedial actions to address any deficiencies in the information security policies, procedures, and practices of the agency;

- procedures for detecting, reporting, and responding to security incidents; and

- plans and procedures to ensure continuity of operations for information systems that support the operations and assets of the agency.

In addition, agencies must produce an annually updated inventory of major information systems (including major national security systems) operated by the agency or under its control, which includes an identification of the interfaces between each system and all other systems or networks, including those not operated by or under the control of the agency.

FISMA also requires each agency to report annually to OMB, selected congressional committees, and the Comptroller General on the adequacy of its information security policies, procedures, practices, and compliance with requirements. In addition, agency heads are required to report annually the results of their independent evaluations to OMB, except to the extent that an evaluation pertains to a national security system; then only a summary and assessment of that portion of the evaluation needs to be reported to OMB.

Responsibilities of Inspectors General

Under FISMA, the inspector general for each agency shall perform an independent annual evaluation of the agency's information security program and practices. The evaluation should include testing of the effectiveness of information security policies, procedures, and practices of a representative subset of agency systems. In addition, the evaluation must include an assessment of the compliance with the act and any related information security policies, procedures, standards, and guidelines. For agencies without an inspector general, evaluations of non-national security systems must be performed by an independent external auditor. Evaluations related to national security systems are to be performed by an entity designated by the agency head.

Responsibilities of the National Institute of Standards and Technology

Under FISMA, the National Institute of Standards and Technology (NIST) is tasked with developing, for systems other than for national security, standards and guidelines that must include, at a minimum: (1) standards to be used by all agencies to categorize all their information and information systems based on the objectives of providing appropriate levels of information security according to a range of risk levels; (2) guidelines recommending the types of information and information systems to be included in each category; and (3) minimum information security requirements for information and information systems in each category. NIST must also develop a definition of and guidelines for detection and handling of information security incidents.

The law also assigns other information security functions to NIST including:

- providing technical assistance to agencies on elements such as compliance with the standards and guidelines, and the detection and handling of information security incidents;

- evaluating private-sector information security policies and practices and commercially available information technologies to assess potential application by agencies;

- evaluating security policies and practices developed for national security systems to assess their potential application by agencies; and

- conducting research, as needed, to determine the nature and extent of information security vulnerabilities and techniques for providing cost-effective information security.

In addition, FISMA requires NIST to prepare an annual report on activities undertaken during the previous year, and planned for the coming year, to carry out responsibilities under the act.

Appendix III: Comments from the Department of Homeland Security

U.S. Department of Homeland Security
Washington, DC 20528

Homeland Security

September 16, 2011

Gregory C. Wilshusen
Director, Information Technology
U.S. Government Accountability Office
4441 G Street, NW
Washington, DC 20548

Re: Draft Report GAO-11-639, "Information Security: Weaknesses Continue Amid New
         Federal Efforts to Implement Requirements"

Dear Mr. Wilshusen:

Thank you for the opportunity to review and comment on this draft report. The U.S. Department
of Homeland Security (DHS) appreciates the U.S. Government Accountability Office's (GAO's)
work in planning and conducting its review and issuing this report.

Although the report contains no recommendations for DHS, the Department is pleased to note
the report's acknowledgement of several DHS efforts to improve the cybersecurity posture of
federal agencies. These include the discussion of challenges faced by the Chief Information
Officers and Chief Information Security Officers from the 24 major federal agencies as well as
the launch of "CyberStat" review sessions.

The "Cyber Stat" sessions help to ensure agency leadership accountability for improved
cybersecurity and assist agencies in driving progress with respect to key strategic enterprise
cybersecurity capabilities. DHS will continue to support its federal agency partners as they
improve their individual cybersecurity postures and the posture of the federal enterprise as a
whole.

Again, thank you for the opportunity to review and comment on this draft report. Technical comments have been submitted under separate cover. We look forward to working with you on future cybersecurity issues.

Sincerely,

Jim H. Crumpacker
Director
Departmental GAO/OIG Liaison Office

2

Appendix IV: GAO Contact and Staff Acknowledgments

GAO Contact

Gregory C. Wilshusen, (202) 512-6244, wilshuseng@gao.gov

Staff Acknowledgments

In addition to the individual named above, Anjalique Lawrence (Assistant Director), Larry Crosland, Season Dietrich, Jennifer Franks, Nancy Glover, Min Hyun, Alina J. Johnson, Mary Marshall, Lee McCracken, Minette Richardson, and Jayne Wilson made key contributions to this report.